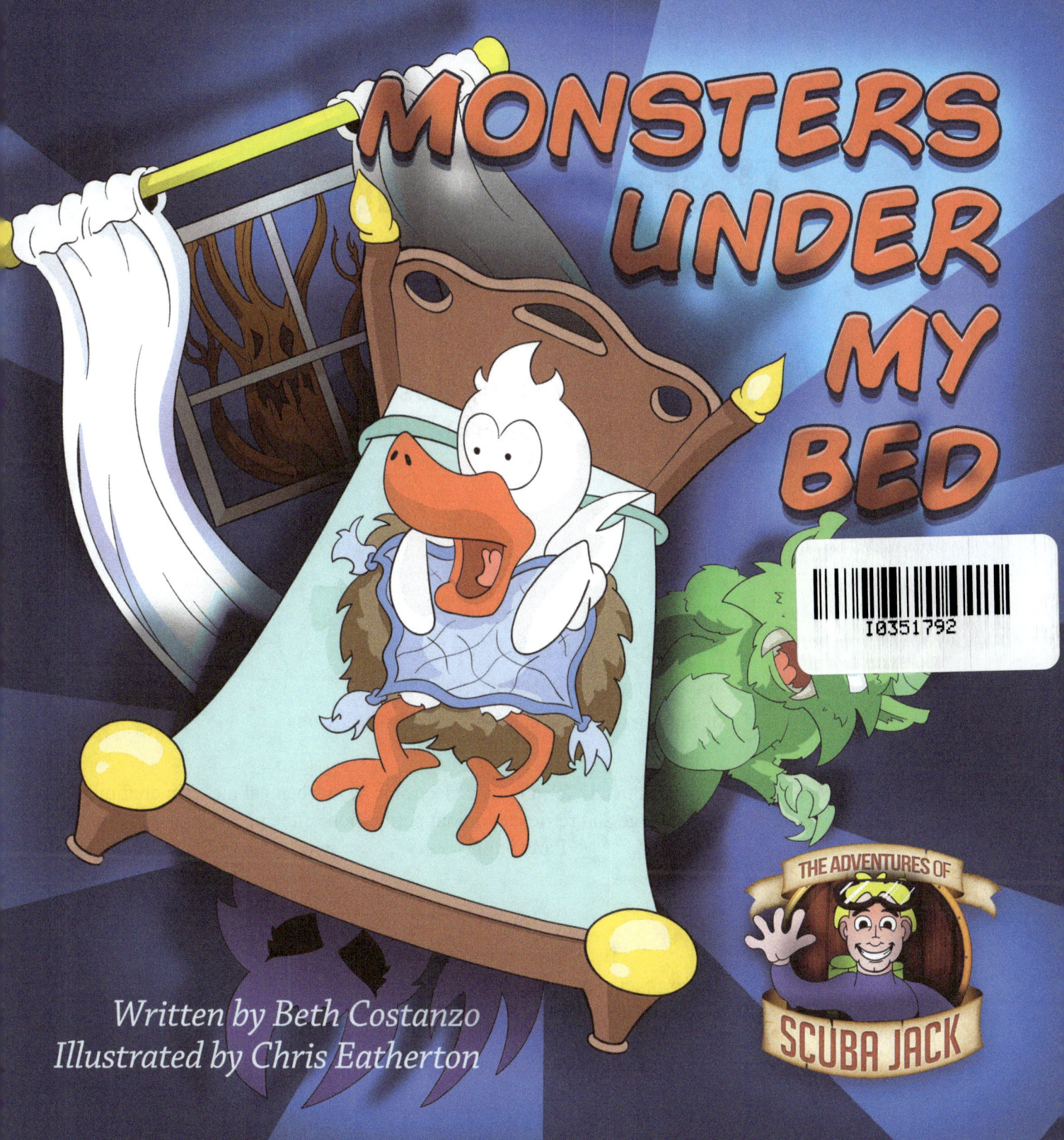

There's a Monster in My Bedroom!

Written by Beth Costanzo
Illustrated by Chris Eatherton

There's a Monster in My Bedroom!

Copyright ©2016 by Beth Constanzo

All rights reserved. Published in the United States

No part of this book may be reproduced in any form by any electronic or mechanical means including photo-copying, recording, or information storage and retrieval without permission of the publisher and International Parts Supply

ISBN:

First Print September 2016

Printed in the United States of America

10 9 8 7 6 5 4 3 2 1

This book is dedicated to my son Salvi Costanzo whose incredible imagination is something beautiful to behold.

It was time for bed.

Paco brushed his teeth and put on his pajamas.

Professor Galaxy walked Paco to his bedroom and read him his favorite Adventures of Scuba Jack bed time story, The Lonely Lobster and tucked him into bed.

Paco closed his eyes and all of a sudden heard a scratching on his window.

"Oh no, it's a monster! PROFESSOR!"

The Professor walked in and found Paco holding on tight to his teddy bear.

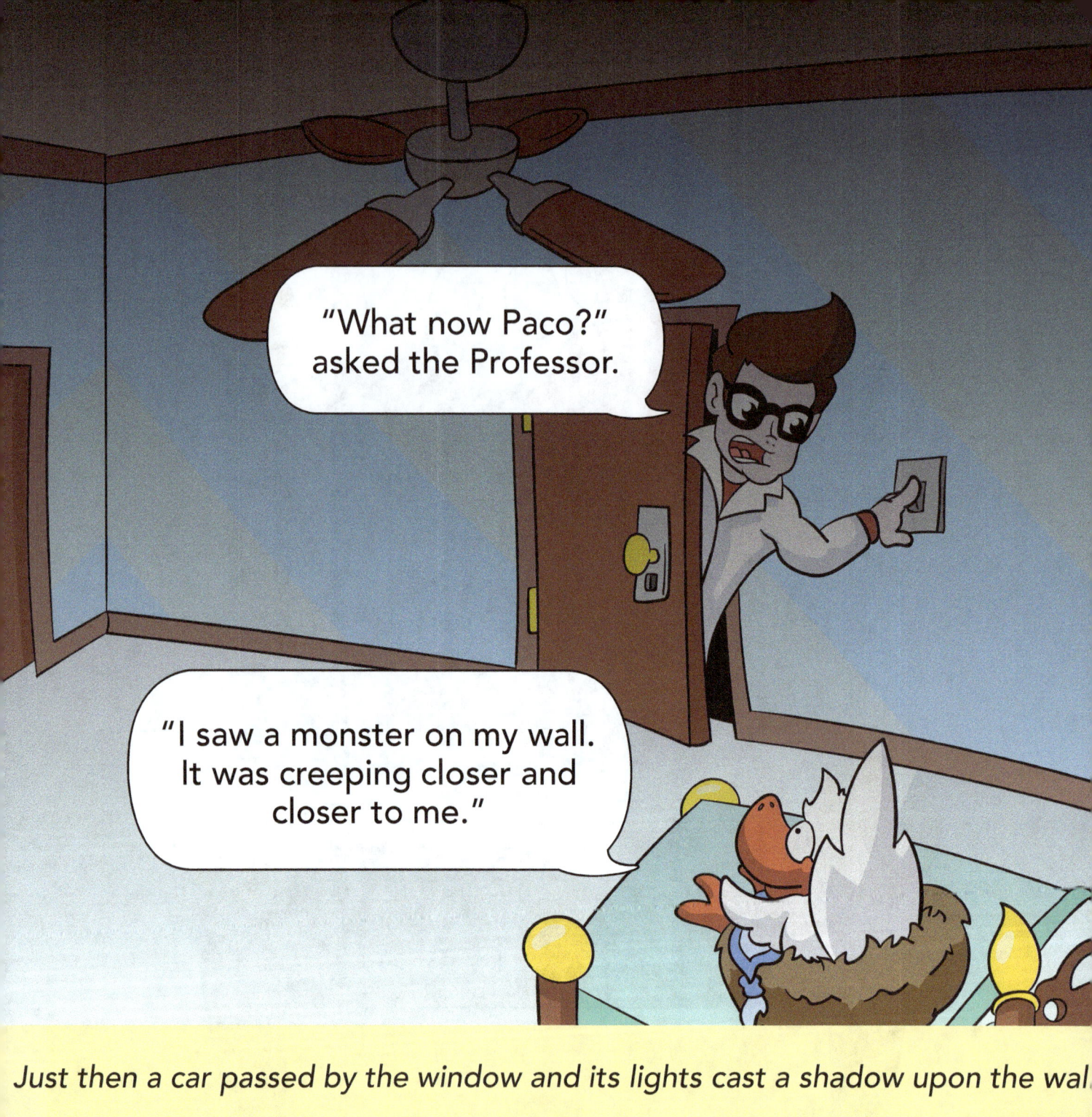

Just then a car passed by the window and its lights cast a shadow upon the wall.

Thirty minutes had passed and the Professor was pleasantly amused by the new crystal he had discovered at the beach the day before.

Paco screamed so loud that it frightened the Professor and he fell off his chair.

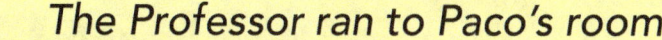

Paco finally fell asleep and was no longer afraid of monsters in his room.

ADDITIONAL BOOKS & RESOURCES AVAILABLE AT
ADVENTURESOF**SCUBAJACK**.COM

BETH COSTANZO
AUTHOR

www.ingramcontent.com/pod-product-compliance
Lightning Source LLC
Chambersburg PA
CBHW060428010526
44118CB00017B/2406